Careers For
Hands-On Types

Interviews by Russell Shorto

Photographs by Edward Keating and Carrie Boretz

CHOICES
The Millbrook Press
Brookfield, Connecticut

Produced in association with Agincourt Press.

Choices Editor: Megan Liberman

Photographs by Edward Keating, except: Catherine Thompson (Jim Berry),
Margaret Ellis (Lynn Delaney Saunders), Sarah Gavaghan (Carrie Boretz),
Deborah Wardwell (Carrie Boretz), Steven Mazur (Carrie Boretz),
Martha Lipton (Carrie Boretz), John Lindemann (Carrie Boretz).

Library of Congress Cataloging-in-Publication Data

Shorto, Russell.
Careers for hands-on types/interviews by Russell Shorto,
photographs by Edward Keating and Carrie Boretz.

p.   cm. — (Choices)
Includes bibliographic references and index.

Summary: People who work with their hands, including a tailor, film
editor, and masseuse, describe what they do in their jobs, how they
got there, and what others would need to get a similar job.

ISBN 1-56294-065-1

1. Vocational guidance — United States — Juvenile literature.
2. Skilled labor — United States — Juvenile literature.
3. Artisans — United States — Interviews.
[1. Occupations.   2. Vocational guidance.]
I. Keating, Edward, ill.   II. Boretz, Carrie, ill.
III. Title.   IV. Series: Choices (Brookfield, Conn.)
HF5381.2.S525   1992   91-47146
331.7'94 — dc20

Contents

Introduction

In this book, fourteen people who work in hands-on fields talk about their careers — what their work involves, how they got started, and what they like (and dislike) about it. They tell you things you should know before beginning a career working with your hands and show you how being good with your hands can lead to many different types of jobs.

Many of the people featured in this book use their hands in artistic careers, such as glass artist, graphic artist, and jewelry designer. Others — such as the masonry restorer, the cabinetmaker, and the bookbinder — work as craftsmen. Still others, including the tailor and the hat designer, use their hands in fashion-related careers. And some use their hands in less obvious ways, such as the videotape editor, the chef, and the masseuse.

The fourteen careers described here are just the beginning, so don't limit your sights. At the end of this book, you'll find short descriptions of a dozen more careers you may want to explore, as well as suggestions on how to get more information. There are many business opportunities for people with agile hands. If you like working with your hands, you'll find a wide range of career choices open to you.

Joan E. Storey, M.B.A., M.S.W.
Series Career Consultant

"You have to envision every step if you want a piece to work out right."

DAVID SCOTT

CABINETMAKER

Norwalk, Connecticut

WHAT I DO:

I build custom-made cabinets and furniture. Much of my work is commissioned by designers and architects, but I also get work through referrals by previous customers. I build cabinets of just about every description — television cabinets, stereo cabinets, file cabinets, and cabinets for coats and jackets. I also build bookcases, tables, and other furniture.

I work in a section of a warehouse where I have three rooms: a main room, where the machines and tools are kept; a side room, where I store most of my wood; and an office, where I keep projects in progress.

Part of my skill in this business is helping people figure out what they want. Sometimes customers come to me knowing exactly what

David planes a board for a stereo cabinet he's building.

they want. Other times all they know is that they want something to hold the television. In those cases, I'll give them pictures of different furniture styles — French, Chinese, whatever. Then, once they've chosen a style they like, I'll do a working drawing of the piece, and we'll come to an agreement on price. There are always little refinements, such as the type and quality of the wood, the finish, and the construction. These refinements cost more, just like extras on a car.

I have my own business, but occasionally I collaborate on a job. For example, if I'm building a large bookcase or a large cabinet, I might work with someone else, because if I did it myself it might take months. I also send furniture out to upholsterers or to artists for ornamentation work. Some customers, however, have a romantic

David sights down a board to see whether it's true.

notion about "the craftsman," and they want everything done by the same person. For these people, I do all the work myself.

These clients don't realize that most furniture has always been built as a collaborative effort. For instance, not all Chippendale furniture was carved by Thomas Chippendale himself. Most of it was designed by Chippendale, but the actual work was usually done by several different craftsmen.

HOW I GOT STARTED:

I did construction work while I was in college and for a few years after. During that time, I got a sense of the construction business, but I didn't find the work very challenging. Then one day I decided to build a set of bookcases for my father, and I realized that I didn't really have the skills. I had never taken a shop class in school nor had any real carpentry training. So I read a lot about carpentry and watched carpenters and cabinetmakers at work.

I got a series of part-time and full-time jobs working for carpenters and taught myself the business as I went along. Eventually I got into doing repairs, and that was invaluable experience. Taking old furniture apart and putting it back together again is a great way to learn.

HOW I FEEL ABOUT IT:

I dream about my work. I'm always picturing in my head what I'll be doing the next day. You have to envision every step if you want a piece to work out right. But there are also times when I hate it. There are days when the wood won't do what I want, or when I realize that I've bought the wrong kind of wood for the job and now I'm stuck with it. Repairing broken pieces can also be a problem, because it means matching new wood to old wood, and that can be very difficult. Then there are jobs that take a lot longer than I thought they would. Every once in a while I spend three days on something I thought would take three hours.

WHAT YOU SHOULD KNOW:
There are plenty of books that have projects you can work on. Try a few and see how you like it. Also look into college programs in artistry or woodworking. You can apprentice for a carpenter or cabinetmaker, but you have to be pretty good even to work as an apprentice.

If you're not coming out of a college program, you might try a job in a furniture factory. Working there will give you an idea of the equipment and techniques involved in furniture construction, and that's a good way to start. You might be making restaurant tables by the hundreds, which can get boring, but you'll learn production techniques.

You'll make about $10 to $15 an hour in a factory. As a skilled carpenter or cabinetmaker, however, you might make $20 to $30 an hour. The more you know, the more you can make.

David tightens a line of screws by hand.

"I use the same techniques that medieval artists used to make stained glass."

CATHERINE THOMPSON

GLASS ARTIST

Seattle, Washington

WHAT I DO:

I'm a glass painter. I work in stained glass, and I also paint blown-glass vases. All the works I create are high-end, fine-art pieces, which retail for between $2,500 and $5,000 each.

I work in my studio with an assistant who does most of the preparatory work, such as the cutting and leading of the glass. I do the design, color selection, and painting. Right now I'm working on several projects, including a stained glass display. It includes four panels, each of which is two-feet square and tells the story of one of Aesop's fables.

My style is reminiscent of medieval stained glass. I think the best work in stained glass was done around the twelfth century, and that's where my heart is.

Catherine holds up one of her finished hand-painted vases.

Medieval stained glass was very symbolic and spiritual, and that appeals to me.

In painting vases, I use the same general techniques that medieval artists used to make stained glass. First, I sketch a drawing on the outside of the vase, which serves as a guide for the paint. The actual painting, however, is done on the inside.

After I finish the painting, I erase the drawing on the outside and fire the piece in a kiln, or pottery oven. When that's done, I sometimes apply a layer of transparent color enamel, which gives the glass a tint much like that of an old photo.

HOW I GOT STARTED:

I first developed an interest in glass painting while I studied art in college. Then I started working in glass as part of an internship program at Evergreen

11

Catherine works on a new design for a vase.

College, in Olympia, Washington. Afterwards, I decided to pursue glass painting as a career.

In the beginning, I had to supplement my income with other part-time work. For a while I taught at the Pilchuck Glass School in Stanwood, Washington, which is the premier glass school in the country. In the last two years, however, my career has turned a corner, and now I can make my living entirely from my art.

HOW I FEEL ABOUT IT:

It's exciting to be in a field that's experiencing a rebirth. There has been a great resurgence of interest in glass art over the last twenty years. There are graduate programs in glass art now, as well as a network of galleries around the country that show the work of glass artists.

I feel very lucky because I really enjoy what I do, and not everyone I know can say that.

WHAT YOU SHOULD KNOW:
If you love expressing yourself through creative outlets, glass art can be a wonderful field to go into. Perseverance is 90 percent of what you need. If you keep at it, your work will eventually find its place in the world.

It's a difficult way to make a living, though. As a fairly successful glass painter, I sold $32,000 worth of art last year, but I also had a lot of expenses. I wouldn't go into this work for the money, but it does have other benefits that other jobs don't have. I love what I'm doing, for instance, so I don't have to spend a lot of money amusing myself outside of work.

Catherine draws guidelines for the paint.

"In this age of disposable goods, I make books that will last for two hundred years."

JOHN GREENAWALD

BOOKBINDER

Washington, D.C.

WHAT I DO:
I use traditional methods and materials to bind books by hand. In this age of disposable goods, I make books that will last for two hundred years. I also apply the same hand-tooling techniques to leather. My company produces such high-end leather goods as desk sets, picture frames, photo albums, atlases, and dictionaries.

Our products are sold all over the world. We have customers in Germany, the Middle East, and on Fifth Avenue. We also do work for the White House. And we have a New York business office that caters to our corporate accounts.

High-quality, hand-bound books are made very differently from mass-produced books. A book is made of very large sheets of paper that are

John embosses the Presidential seal on a hand-bound book.

folded over again and again. These folded sheets are called signatures.

In traditional binding, you hand-sew the signatures together before trimming the pages to make them all the same size. Then you sew the signatures to the binding. Everything is done by hand.

With mass-produced books, on the other hand, all the work is done mechanically. The signatures are sewn together and trimmed by machine, and then they are simply glued to their bindings.

All books used to be hand-sewn so they could last for hundreds of years. But once books began to be bound by machine, the quality dropped. As a result, a book that was made two hundred years ago, before industrialization, is typically in better condition than a book made sixty years ago.

John inspects some hand-marbled endpapers.

HOW I GOT STARTED:

I started in this business as a part-time salesman while I was still in college studying music. In order to be more effective at my job, I learned about the history and techniques of bookbinding. I also spent a great deal of time in the bindery, watching the binders at work restoring the rare book collection of the Army & Navy Club. The restoration took a year and a half, and I learned a tremendous amount about the craft by observing the process.

I also spent some time researching hand-marbled endpapers, and I developed a process by which several sheets of paper could be hand-marbled at the same time. Eventually all my research and hard work paid off. I'm now a bookbinder myself as well as treasurer of the company, and it all came out of my desire to learn the business so that I could sell the product better.

HOW I FEEL ABOUT IT:

I've always wanted to do something inventive and expressive. Originally I wanted to be a singer, which led me to have a negative attitude about this work in the beginning. But once I became more involved with it, I realized how creative and exciting this field could be. I work a terrific number of hours, but I love it. I find it fascinating to produce something that will last well beyond my lifetime.

WHAT YOU SHOULD KNOW:
There are two areas of traditional bookbinding in which jobs are available. One is creative bookbinding, and that's where I've carved my niche. Creative bookbinding is an art form in which the binding itself is the art: the workmanship of the leather, the sewing, the marbling. Fortunately for our business, fine, hand-bound books are increasing in popularity and demand.

The other area where jobs are available is in book conservation, especially the technical end. Book conservators use advanced scientific techniques to repair and restore old and damaged books. Millions of important old books must be restored within the next decade if they are going to be saved, so there's an enormous amount of work to be done.

In general, because of the resurgence of interest in traditional bookbinding, there are opportunities today that weren't available five or ten years ago. But the business has also changed. I learned bookbinding as an apprentice, but people interested in pursuing hand bookbinding today need a research background. The Library of Congress has a wonderful internship in bookbinding and conservation. You could write to them for information.

As far as the pay goes, there is some money to be made in this field. The binders on my staff earn about $18 an hour. A research position as a certified book conservator can also pay well.

John holds up a copy of the Presidential seal.

"My jewelry has a very distinctive style."

MARGARET ELLIS

JEWELRY DESIGNER

Nashville, Tennessee

WHAT I DO:

I design jewelry that is sold in high-fashion boutiques — the kinds of stores that will sell a thousand-dollar blouse. My jewelry is also seen in fashion magazines, such as *Mademoiselle* and *Vogue*. And it's worn on the television programs "All My Children" and "Another World." I usually get credit in magazines, but rarely on television shows.

I have my own business, which I run with my husband. I do all the design work, and he manages the business end of things. I also have a staff of five people, who help make the jewelry. We make it all entirely by hand, which is very rare. We make all kinds of jewelry, but earrings are our biggest sellers.

I design a new collection for each of five different

Margaret specializes in making hoop earrings like these.

marketing seasons: summer, early fall, fall, holiday, and spring. For each season, there's a trade show in New York, which is a lot of fun. You need new designs for each show if you want to get people's attention. But you also have to be careful to maintain some continuity so that buyers can get a sense of your style.

My jewelry has a very distinctive style. Usually people who are familiar with my work can recognize my designs in an ad. I've developed a look with a lot of hoops in it. I also do some jewelry that involves layered metal. I might design a series of layered metal jewelry for one season and then bring it back later with stones added. People can look at the pieces and see an evolution.

HOW I GOT STARTED:

Before I got into jewelry design, I taught junior high

Margaret makes all of her jewelry by hand.

school for eighteen years. I enjoyed teaching, but it was too straight for me. I had always wanted to do something glamorous and artistic. I loved fashion jewelry, so I decided to try designing some myself. I did a series of samples and went right to New York to try to sell them.

I only sold a few things, but it gave me the confidence to continue.

When I came back to Nashville, I decided to start my own jewelry business in my home, and I hired a couple of people to help me. We were all amateurs, but we learned as we went along.

Eventually we took over the entire house, and my husband said, "What is happening to our life?" That's when we moved the business to a real work studio.

HOW I FEEL ABOUT IT:

I love being creative and doing my own thing. I've always been a very unorthodox person, and this job allows me to be a little bit weird. I also like the way we do business. We don't see it as just a way to make money. We see it as an adventure. I have the freedom to express myself, and so do the people who work for me.

WHAT YOU SHOULD KNOW:

I believe that people can do whatever they want to as long as they're really focused about it. I was a forty-year-old junior high school teacher in Nashville, Tennessee.

I knew nothing about the jewelry business. But I got into it anyway.

The key is to know what you want. Then you have to set definite goals for yourself and pursue them. Ultimately, you have to realize that every issue in life is a spiritual issue. You have to figure out whether what you want to do will be good for you and good for the world.

If you work for someone creating jewelry, you usually get paid by the piece. If you work fast, you might earn about $400 a week. If you start your own business, however, you have to get by on next to nothing for a while. My business provides enough for my husband and me to live comfortably, but we're not flying to France on the Concorde. Fortunately, we're not really hung up about money.

Margaret hammers a metal bracelet into shape.

"I teach my students to do the same kind of work that I've been doing for over forty years."

MARION ANDERSON
TAILOR

New York, New York

WHAT I DO:

I'm a custom tailor by profession, but I also teach tailoring and operate my own school, the Manhattanville Needle Trade School. Teaching is my full-time job, but I still spend about 20 percent of my time doing men's custom tailoring. I keep my equipment in a shop at the school, and private clients come to me there.

There are several stages in making a custom-tailored men's suit. First, the client and I select the fabric. Then I take measurements, produce patterns, and do a series of fittings until the suit fits perfectly. It takes me two full days to produce a single suit.

I teach my students to do the same kind of work that I've been doing for over forty years. There have been considerable changes in the

It takes Marion two full days to make a single men's suit.

garment industry since the dawn of computers. Today computers are used to design patterns, and computerized sewing machines perform tasks that were once done manually. These changes, however, apply mostly to mass production. Individual custom-made clothes, like the ones I make, are still produced the old-fashioned way — by hand. And this is the method I teach.

My curriculum provides a foundation for novices who want to enter the industry. It covers the four divisions of the trade: cutting room operations, which include measurement, pattern design, and garment cutting; machine operations, which include finishing seam edges and making button holes and hems; hand sewing, which involves learning the various stitches; and pressing, which includes both hand pressing and machine pressing.

The students at my school also learn about textiles. It's important to have an understanding of fibers in terms of type, construction, and origin because the whole process of tailoring starts with the fibers.

HOW I GOT STARTED:

I majored in tailoring in high school. After graduation, I worked in a variety of jobs in the industry, in custom tailoring and alterations as well as in manufacturing and mass production.

After fifteen years in the business, I decided I wanted to teach. In order to become qualified, I studied industrial education and earned my bachelor's degree. Then I became the first African-American to be licensed by the City of New York as a men's clothing manufacturing teacher. I've been teaching for thirty years.

HOW I FEEL ABOUT IT:

I like working with people, and teaching allows me to do that. I really enjoy sharing my knowledge with my students. I also get a great deal of satisfaction from seeing a finished product. That was one of the things that stimulated my interest in high school — making a garment and having people admire my work. It's still very important to me today.

Marion advises one of his students on machine sewing.

Marion works on a custom-made suit for a private client.

WHAT YOU SHOULD KNOW:
Today kids don't have the same opportunity that I had — that is, to work as a pre-apprentice. Instead, there are a few programs in which students spend one week in school and the next working on the job. The High School of Fashion in New York City, for instance, has an excellent program that allows kids to do this. We need more programs like it. It also helps to work in the industry in after-school jobs.

I think schooling in the trade is very important. My first job was at a very exclusive custom tailoring company. But while I was there, I realized that many of my co-workers, who had been apprentices, didn't have the same broad background I had gotten from school. In school I was exposed to the whole field, and I was able to adapt to all facets of the industry.

With the proper training, there are many job opportunities available. And they can be profitable as well. You might start out making only $12,000 a year as a tailor, but you can move up rapidly to about $40,000 a year. The salary for a tailoring teacher is around $55,000 a year.

"To me, making hats is like making sculpture."

SARAH GAVAGHAN

HAT DESIGNER

New York, New York

WHAT I DO:

My company creates, engineers, produces, and markets fashionable hats. I have a partner, and we have four people who work for us. We've been in business for three years now. I develop the designs and oversee the production. On average, it takes me between one and three hours to make a hat. My partner sells the hats, pays the bills, and collects unpaid invoices.

We sell to most of the major department stores in New York, such as Saks Fifth Avenue and Bloomingdale's. These stores all have hat departments, but they also have designer floors, which carry more expensive and exclusive merchandise. The designer floors are where most of my hats are sold. We also sell to smaller

Sarah uses many techniques to create unique shapes for her hats.

boutiques that specialize in high fashion. In fact, most of our sales are to these specialty stores.

There is a formal way to make hats, but I never studied millinery, or hat making, so I didn't learn it. Because I'm self-taught, everything I do is unorthodox. I don't have a structured approach, so I'm always look-ing for new shapes and ideas. I let the materials I use dictate the shapes. For instance, with winter hats, designers normally start with a felt body, which they steam and then mold. I don't do that. I take felt, cut it, and then sew it together to make my own shapes. It's an unusual approach, but it has given me my niche in the market.

My design ideas come from everywhere, and I try to find unusual materials to work with. Hats were very popular in the 1940s, when

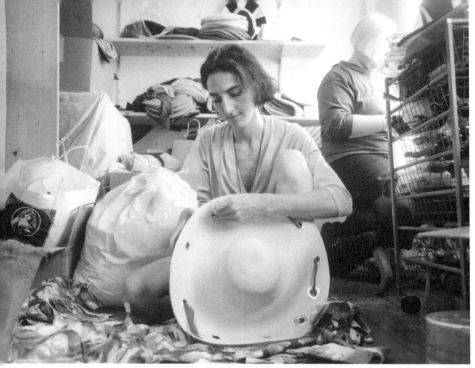

Sarah decorates her hats with ribbons and bows.

there was a lot of interesting material. Today, you don't have the variety you once did.

Selling is a hard push all the time. We do accessory shows in New York three times a year, and we have sales representatives in Los Angeles, Chicago, and Atlanta, who do shows in those areas and send us the orders they receive.

HOW I GOT STARTED:

I went to art college to study sculpture. But while I was in school, I made a hat for a friend, who loved it and told me I should make hats for a living. That sounded like fun, so when I graduated, I decided to start my own hat business. In the beginning, I made a

lot of mistakes. For one, I tried to sell hats for June in June, not realizing that stores buy one season ahead.

Also, in the beginning, I had to sell my hats on consignment — which meant that stores didn't pay me until the hats were sold. If a hat didn't sell, I had to take it back. Slowly, though, stores started to pay me for the hats up front. It took a lot of perseverance to get there, though. I had to wait two years before I really made a living at this.

HOW I FEEL ABOUT IT:

I've always loved sculpture — and to me, making hats is like making sculpture. Also, being in business for myself,

I call my own shots. After working hard for three years, for example, I decided to take two months off and travel. It's a great thing to have that kind of freedom.

I'm often frustrated, however, by the limitations on what I can design if I want those designs to sell. Hat designers have to be very aware of what people will buy if they want to shoot for the mass market. When I first started out, my hats were very artsy and wild. But I've had to tone down my designs because American women aren't comfortable wearing hats. In England, women don't mind being looked at as much, but American women think hats draw too much attention to them. Still, things are changing here, and the field is growing.

WHAT YOU SHOULD KNOW: Some people study millinery for four years, but I don't see why. I think it limits them. Instead, I'd suggest studying fashion while simply taking courses in millinery.

Hat making is a great thing to do, but building up a business takes time. You have to be tenacious. If you start out as a seamstress, doing basic sewing work, you make about $6 an hour. But if you start a business and expand, there's no telling how much money you can make. The sky's the limit, but it takes a long time getting there.

Sarah sews a fold into one of her straw hats.

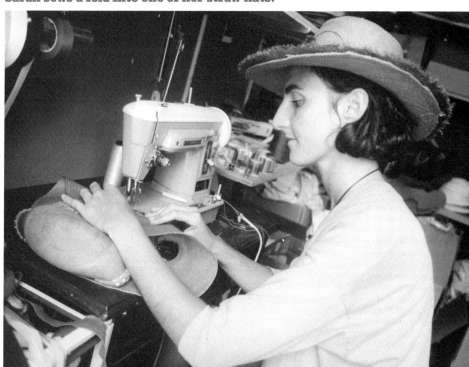

"By saving the architecture of this country, we're saving part of our history."

MICHAEL F. WÜSTNER

MASONRY RESTORER

Washington, D.C.

WHAT I DO:

I restore the masonry facades of buildings. I have my own business, and I employ from six to ten people depending on how much work I have. We restore mostly brick buildings, which works out well because Washington, D.C., happens to be the brick capital of the United States. We don't focus so much on the bricks themselves, however, as on the mortar that holds the bricks together. After about eighty years, mortar begins to deteriorate, and it has to be replaced.

You have to be very careful to use the right mortar, however, because there are differences between modern bricks and older bricks. For modern bricks, which are hard, we generally use cement-based mortar. For older bricks, however, which

Michael replaces some deteriorating mortar.

are softer, we use a mortar made of sand and lime. If you're restoring a house from 1900, for example, you'd use lime-based mortar, which we make by hand because it's no longer commercially available. A cement-based mortar would be too hard, and in time it would break the faces of the bricks.

The colonial English would settle only in those places where they could find sand, lime, and clay — sand and lime to make mortar, clay to make bricks. I just restored a house in Alexandria, Virginia, that dates from 1800. I figured out that the sand was dredged from the river, the lime came from oyster shells, and the clay was dug locally.

Our business comes by word of mouth from people who know that we do high-quality restoration work — that we aren't simply bricklayers. We do historic preservation, and we follow the restoration standards set by the Department of the Interior. And there's one extra thing we do — we take pride in our workmanship.

HOW I GOT STARTED:

I was trained as a cultural anthropologist, but during my fieldwork, I got interested in archaeology. I was especially fascinated by old earthen dwellings, and eventually my interest broadened from how people lived into where people lived as well. About this time, I also began renovating apartments, but I still wasn't sure what I really wanted to do. Then I met an old Italian mason, who pointed out to me how badly the buildings in the area needed to be restored. I went to the library of the National Trust for Historic Preservation and did research on how to restore buildings properly. Then I started my business with a bicycle, a backpack full of tools, and $200.

HOW I FEEL ABOUT IT:

When you learn how to do this well, you're really welcome in neighborhoods

Michael hand-mixes mortar for an old facade.

Michael often needs a scaffold to reach high bricks.

because you renew things. I can be proud of the work I do because I really make things nice. In a small way, the job I do has significance. One of my workers, who doesn't speak much English, once said to me, "My work is really important." I know how he felt. By preserving the architecture of this country, we're saving a part of the history of America, a part of our history as a people.

WHAT YOU SHOULD KNOW:
If you find this work interesting, there are a number of places you can turn to for information. The Department of the Interior produces several pamphlets on different types of restoration work. You can use that information to figure out which sorts of restoration projects interest you. You can also look up the government office in your town or city that deals with the preservation of old buildings — which can often put you in touch with the people in your area who do restoration work. And you can write to the National Trust for Historic Preservation in Washington, D.C.

Pay for restoration work starts at about $7 an hour and goes up to about $15 an hour. After you've been in the business for a number of years, however, you can start your own company and make anywhere from $50,000 to $100,000 a year.

"Cooking is really an art form, and it involves all the senses."

ILANA SARAF

CHEF

San Francisco, California

WHAT I DO:
As the chef and owner of a small restaurant, I plan the menus for lunch and dinner, order the ingredients, and do a lot of the cooking. At lunchtime, I mostly manage the restaurant, but I also help out the lunch cooks on the grill or with the salads. After lunch, I spend the entire afternoon prepping for dinner — chopping vegetables, making sauces, and so on. And finally, during the dinner shift, I'm in the kitchen, cooking.

I like to have a varied menu. We have eight regular entrees, plus specials. We always have one soup, a chicken dish, a seafood dish, and lots of fresh produce. But we change the entire menu at least once a month, and some changes we even make on a daily basis. I design the

Ilana designs her menus around the produce that's in season.

menu around what's in season, because I like to use only the best ingredients. Local suppliers will call and tell me they have wonderful wild berries available, so I'll tell my pastry chef to design a dessert with berries.

Our menu emphasizes French and Mediterranean dishes, but I like to draw on other influences as well, such as Thai and Chinese cooking. Because we're never sure how a new dish will turn out, we test all our new dishes a week before listing them on the menu. We keep altering the ingredients until the taste is just right. Then all the waiters and waitresses try the new dishes so they can describe what they'll be serving.

My job goes beyond food, however, because I'm the owner. I'm responsible for everything that happens here — fixing a leaky sink, playing den mother to the staff,

During the afternoon, Ilana prepares for dinner.

managing the space, and bookkeeping. My days are very long. I start early in the morning, and I get home very late at night smelling of fish and garlic.

HOW I GOT STARTED:

I inherited my interest in food from my grandmother. She had a catering business, and when I was in high school, I worked for her.

In college, though, I was an art major. I thought at the time that I'd probably become an architect, and after graduation I managed an architectural drafting store for a while. Eventually, however, I decided that architecture wasn't for me. I realized that what I really wanted to do was own a restaurant.

When I asked around, people who knew the busi-

ness advised me against cooking school. They told me to work in restaurants instead, and I spent the next six years working in different cooking jobs. Then I found a little restaurant that was being sold, and I bought it.

HOW I FEEL ABOUT IT:

I love the creative part of this work. Cooking is really an art form, and it involves all the senses. When you're working with food, it's not only taste that matters. Colors, smells, and textures are also important. In addition to being delicious, food should always be beautifully presented. And because I'm a painter as well as a chef, I always pay a lot of attention to the look of each dish.

Basically, I like owning my own restaurant. It's incredibly challenging, but it's also very satisfying. You get to work with talented people, and you're constantly increasing your knowledge of food and the craft of cooking. The downside is that owning your own place can be incredibly grueling, and it leaves you almost no free time.

WHAT YOU SHOULD KNOW:
You can go to cooking school to become a chef if you need that kind of structure. The Culinary Institute of America, in upstate New York, is known as an excellent place to learn the craft. Many community colleges also offer very good programs, and they're generally inexpensive. But work experience is important whether or not you have any schooling.

If you want to work in the food business, get any kind of hands-on experience you can. Work at a hotel, a fine restaurant, or even a fast-food place. Do dishwashing, wash lettuce. Any work experience you can get is valuable. You should also go to restaurants and sample different styles of cooking, such as Ethiopian food or Egyptian food.

The pay for a chef depends on where you work. If you work in a hotel, you get union wages, which are much higher than the wages at other restaurants. The average non-union pay in San Francisco for a cook is about $10 per hour. If you work your way up to executive chef in a well-known restaurant, you can make about $30,000 a year. There are celebrity chefs who make a lot more, but they are few and far between.

Ilana experiments with a new entree for her menu.

"I like to look at editing as a poetic job."

PATRICK FILIA

VIDEOTAPE EDITOR

Arlington, Virginia

WHAT I DO:
I work for the NBC affiliate in Washington, D.C., editing videotape for news stories. The cameraman may have shot an hour of tape for a story, but we usually have only a minute or two of airtime available. My job is to select the images that will best tell the story and then combine them into a fluid one-minute piece.

Most of the tape I edit is shot for local stories covered by our reporters. But I also edit network feeds, which are tapes of news stories relayed by satellite from all over the world. These stories come in with a complete voice-over, or with a script for the anchor to read. Feeds tend to be quick stories about such things as a fire burning out of control in California. We usually give

Patrick selects the best images for a one-minute story.

them about thirty seconds of airtime each, as opposed to two minutes for a local story.

There's a lot of technical knowledge and manual skill involved in videotape editing. I use two video machines — one to run the camera tape, and one to edit — as well as monitors for each. The first monitor shows the raw tape, and the second shows the edited version.

Then there's the audio track, which has to combine both the reporter's narration and the background sounds. I use an audio mixer to tone down the background sounds so that they don't interfere with the reporter's voice. One pair of hands — mine — works all three machines at once.

But good editing isn't only a product of technical expertise. There's also a creative aspect to it, called shot selection, which I find far more interesting. Shot selection involves finding the

Patrick pulls a tape from the video library.

I've been a tape and film editor for twenty-five years now. In my career, I've edited everything from news to documentaries to cartoons. I've won two Emmy awards as well as a CINE Golden Eagle award, which is a prestigious honor for documentary excellence.

When I got my first job as a film editor, I didn't know anything about editing. I learned everything on the job. The work was very different in those days when we used only silent, black-and-white film. But it was a good way to learn editing, because there was no audio to distract you, and you only had to focus on the screen.

Things changed a great deal when color and sound were added. At first, the audio was on a separate tape, and you had to synchronize the pictures with the sound, which took a lot of precision. Also, in those days, editing meant cutting the film with a pair of scissors. Once you cut it, you couldn't restore it, so you had to be absolutely sure about each cut. It was like performing surgery — there was no margin for error.

In the late 1970s, however, television news programs began using videotape instead of regular film, which drastically changed the industry.

most dramatic shots that best illustrate a story and then deciding how to pace them. I like to look at editing as a poetic job. Over time, anyone can acquire the technical skills, but the artistic part is something that people are born with.

40

Today, you can rework a piece as often as you like, so you don't have to worry about getting it right the first time. But not everyone uses videotape now. Movies and animated shows, for instance, are still shot on real film, and film editors on those jobs edit the old-fashioned way.

HOW I FEEL ABOUT IT:

I'm an editor by nature. It's the way I think. I enjoy cutting news stories because no two are alike. I also get to work with a lot of interesting people, including editors, producers, and well-known reporters. But creative people can also be difficult because they're often egotistical and temperamental.

WHAT YOU SHOULD KNOW:

To do this work, you need good hand-eye coordination. And if you're going to edit news stories, you should be interested in current events.

As far as training goes, some universities offer courses in television production, of which editing is a part. After you finish school, it's a good idea to start out at a smaller station in a small community. Then, once you have some experience, you can move into a larger market.

This industry is changing rapidly. In a few years, it will probably be quite different.

The large broadcasting companies now prefer to use freelancers rather than hire full-time employees. So young people getting into this business often start as freelancers.

The money at larger stations is good. Right now here in Washington, an experienced editor at a major station can earn a base salary of about $1,000 a week. And there's also overtime available, so you can make even more.

Patrick has to synchronize the sound and pictures.

"In this line of work, you have to keep up with current trends."

DEBORAH WARDWELL

HAIRDRESSER

New York, New York

WHAT I DO:

I own and operate my own beauty salon. We do mostly cuts, perms, and hair coloring. We're a small operation, kind of a neighborhood place, so our clients range from kids to businesspeople to grandmothers.

In this line of work, you have to keep up with current trends, especially if you work in New York, where people are very fashion conscious. I keep up by watching what people wear and how they look. I also look for new styles in fashion and hair magazines and then try to duplicate them.

Actually, I'm sometimes part of the fashion industry myself. Many top fashion magazines are located in New York, so there's often a lot of work doing freelance styling for fashion shoots. That's

Deborah specializes in cuts but also does perms and color.

styling, as opposed to cutting. Styling is a specialized thing. Occasionally people will come into my shop for styling for special parties or events, but most of what we do here are cuts.

HOW I GOT STARTED:

I entered beauty school right out of high school. Beauty school lasts for about a year, and it teaches you all the things you need to know for your state-board exam. After beauty school, I did an apprenticeship before I got a job as a full-fledged stylist. After working for a few years in a big salon, I decided to go into business for myself. I've had my own shop for four years now.

HOW I FEEL ABOUT IT:

Every time you start working on a new haircut, it's like an artist starting a new drawing. This is an aesthetic job, and that's part of the fun.

You look at the person, the shape of his or her face and so on. Then you try to come up with something to make that person look beautiful.

Sometimes this job can be difficult because clients want you to make them look like models they see in magazines. They don't always realize that not every style will work for every face or with every head of hair. If someone asks for a cut that I think will be a disaster, I try to counsel him or her against it. If the person still insists on having it done, I suggest trying another salon. For the most part, however, people listen to my advice, and together we come up with a cut that looks good.

It can also be hard dealing with the public all day long. You always have to be friendly and charming, and you have to remain sensitive to people's likes and dislikes. After talking to ten people, however, and being cheerful with each one of them, I don't always feel cheerful anymore.

WHAT YOU SHOULD KNOW:
To become a professional hairdresser, you need to attend a beauty school in order to get licensed by your state. You don't need a college degree, though, and in many states you can get your beauty certificate while you're still in high school. But you do need that license. Where you go to beauty

Deborah sells hair-care products at her salon.

Deborah makes sure that the front is evenly cut.

school isn't important. All that really matters is that you get licensed.

In beauty school, you learn basic cuts, manicures, and facials as well as a little anatomy and chemistry, all of which prepare you for the licensing exam. And you also get some hands-on experience giving haircuts to the public.

After you get your license, you should continue your education as an apprentice or assistant to an established hairdresser. Most big salons have an apprenticeship program. You might do shampoos and help out the hairdressers in exchange for night classes in haircutting. An apprenticeship can last from one to two years, depending on how quickly you learn.

You have to like people to do this work. And you have to be creative and have a good eye. An art background can be very useful, so I would suggest taking art classes in high school.

The money in this field varies tremendously. As an apprentice, you're paid minimum wage plus tips. Your first year as a stylist, you might make $13,000. But after working for about ten years in a place like New York, you can expect to make $50,000 a year if you're good. And in the best salons, you can make over $100,000 a year.

"Some people don't mind spending more on the frame than on the artwork itself."

STEVEN MAZUR

PICTURE FRAMER

New York, New York

WHAT I DO:

I specialize in conservation picture framing, which means that I prepare a piece of artwork so it can be preserved indefinitely. When I frame a picture, I use only materials that won't age or damage the artwork. I use acid-free matting, for example, as well as protective plexiglass that filters out the sun's harmful rays. The hinges I use are Japanese rice paper hinges, which are the best hinges for preservation.

When clients bring me pictures to be framed, my first job is to determine how they want the artwork presented. Do they want a conventional frame, or some sort of plexiglass encasement? Should the frame be bold so that it spices up the artwork, or should it be very plain? Once these decisions are made, I work out the pricing.

Usually a person who comes in with a $20 piece of art doesn't want to spend $200 framing it, but some people don't flinch at that, because a really good frame can turn an otherwise dull piece of art into something really special. Some people don't mind spending more money on the frame than on the artwork itself.

I use many different techniques in my work depending on the type of piece I'm framing. For instance, if it's a poster, I might dry mount it and use glass. If it's a canvas, how-ever, I'll stretch it on a stretcher. Usually, you don't put glass over the front of a canvas, but you do put a nice big frame around it. And whatever materials I'm using, of course, have to be sized to fit the artwork.

Steven completes a frame with matting and a pane of glass.

Steven carefully measures a piece of artwork.

HOW I GOT STARTED:

I worked in a number of jobs before doing this, but none of them really appealed to me. I've always been good at working with my hands and working with tools, so one day I answered an ad for a framer in the newspaper. I got the job and started as a kind of apprentice, working under careful observation. There are a lot of do's and don't's to learn in this field, so you have to be on probation in the beginning.

As I gained more experience, though, I began working with more expensive pieces of art. I also worked my way into selling frames, which mostly involves coordinating the frames with the artwork. That's an especially interesting aspect of the business because there's a lot of creativity involved. I've been framing for almost four years now, and I really like it.

HOW I FEEL ABOUT IT:

It's exciting when somebody comes in with a really valuable piece of artwork. We once got to frame a $500,000 Matisse. It's incredible to work with a piece of paper that's only ten inches by twelve inches and know that it's worth half-a-million dollars. But I don't want to mislead anybody. This isn't a glamorous job. It can be dull, just fitting one picture after another into a frame.

WHAT YOU SHOULD KNOW:
To get into this field, you should be interested in art. You'll learn that there's a lot of imagination involved — that framing artwork is an art in itself. Obviously, you also have to be good with your hands. And you need to be very precise. You're dealing with valuable materials, and if you're off by a sixteenth of an inch on a cut, you'll have to scrap that piece and start all over again.

The only way to learn this business is by working for somebody who knows it well.

Go through the yellow pages, call up framing stores, and ask whether they have any openings. They'll train you to do what they do.

Not many people realize this, but there are a lot of related fields an experienced framer can get into. You can work part time as a picture hanger, for instance. You'd be surprised how many people call up just to have someone come over and hang their art. And by learning more about art, you can move into the gallery world.

A picture framer working at a good frame shop usually starts in the neighborhood of $20,000 a year. Salaries go up from there, and you can also make commissions. But if you want to make a lot of money, you'll have to start your own business.

Steven tightens the hinges on a framed picture.

"I like to break the rules and make people laugh."

MARTHA LIPTON

GRAPHIC ARTIST

New York, New York

WHAT I DO:

I work as a freelance graphic designer, and I hire other freelancers when I need help. I've designed everything from packaging for children's toys to ads for banks and television shows. Right now I'm designing a wedding invitation, and I'm working on a logo and packaging for party goods.

Some graphic designers merely implement a client's ideas. Others come up with a concept and then see it through. I tend to design entire campaigns, because I like to participate in long-term projects. People hire me to come up with concepts, because they know I'll have a lot of different ideas, and they know I enjoy the challenge.

Unlike most graphic designers, I don't have a degree in graphic design. But

Martha picks out colors for a toy package she is designing.

I think that my ignorance of some of the classic techniques actually works for me. I was trained in the fine arts, where there are no rules. I go where my mind and heart lead me.

As a result, I take an unconventional approach to graphic design. I like to break the rules and make people laugh, so I use a lot of humor in my work. For example, my business card comes attached to a tea bag. People never forget my name, and I always leave a smile on their faces.

HOW I GOT STARTED:

I have nice handwriting and I draw well, so I was often asked to make signs and posters in high school. I never planned on becoming a graphic artist, however. In college, I got my degree in fine arts and romance languages.

After I graduated, I wasn't sure what I wanted to do, so

Martha works on a poster in her studio.

I went to work making signs for stores around town. One of these stores then asked me to design a newspaper ad for them. An ad salesman for a weekly paper noticed it and offered me a job designing ads and working on the layout of the paper. I worked there for a few years; then I left to go out on my own.

HOW I FEEL ABOUT IT:
For the most part, I love what I do. Occasionally I get jobs that don't really excite me, but I try to make every job special. And when I do get one of those really great jobs working with wonderful photographers and illustrators, it's a very rewarding experience.

It's also satisfying to have one's work appreciated. I used to do illustrations for a daily newspaper, for example, and once I got a letter from a writer thanking me for the illustration that accompanied his story. That kind of applause makes it all worthwhile. It feels great to create something special and then get more than just a paycheck in return.

Design work can be very challenging. You never know who you're going to run into or what they'll throw at you.

I really think of myself as a problem solver, and that stimulates me. I like knowing that I can deal with both the Wall Street guy and the MTV kid.

There are always problems, though. I once did a beautiful piece for a famous ballet company, and the printer ruined the job. That's only one of my horror stories.

WHAT YOU SHOULD KNOW:
I think anybody who goes into graphic design should know about computers, because computers are where this business is going. They save a lot of time and money in typesetting, design, and almost every other facet of the business. You might also consider learning about computer animation, which is a lot of fun and a field that's still evolving.

If you're interested in this work, visit a design studio, or try to get a summer internship so that you can see what goes on behind the scenes. You can also write to your local chapter of the Graphic Artists Guild. They may be able to help you.

The money is really unpredictable. You can make anywhere from $12,000 a year on up, depending on the skills you have. If you really want to make money, however, do work for corporate clients. It's not the most creative end of the industry, but it pays the best.

Martha works on a sketch for an advertisement.

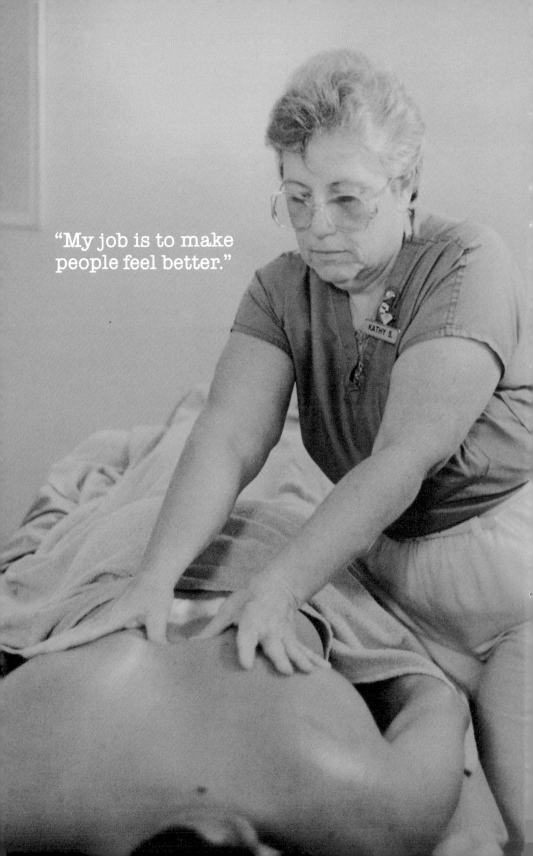

"My job is to make
people feel better."

KATHY STEIN

MASSEUSE

Miami, Florida

WHAT I DO:
My job is to make people feel better, which involves more than just massage. I also give other treatments, including hydrotherapy, reflexology, aromatherapy, and fango.

I work at an international spa that's modeled after an ancient health resort in Italy. The goal here is to reduce stress and improve fitness. Most of our guests come to us in order to relax while they're learning to exercise regularly and eat properly.

Massage is an important part of our program. It's beneficial for the circulatory system, gets rid of toxins, and of course reduces tension. We do two basic kinds of massage here — Swedish massage and shiatsu. Swedish massage is a soothing type of massage that relies on an even stroke,

while shiatsu is deeper and more penetrating.

The other treatments we offer are also designed to relieve tension and heal the body. Hydrotherapy is a water treatment during which the guest is put into a tub with strong water jets. The pressure from the jets helps improve circulation while relieving tension, stress, and sore muscles.

Reflexology is a treatment of the feet. People have more nerve endings in their feet than in all the rest of their bodies. By massaging the feet at strategic points, I can clear up problems in other parts of the body and get everything back to a healthy state.

Aromatherapy is a treatment that dates back to ancient Babylon. It's a massage that employs fragrant oils to foster serenity, therapy, and vitality. If a guest is in need of relaxation,

Kathy gives a Swedish massage to one of the spa's guests.

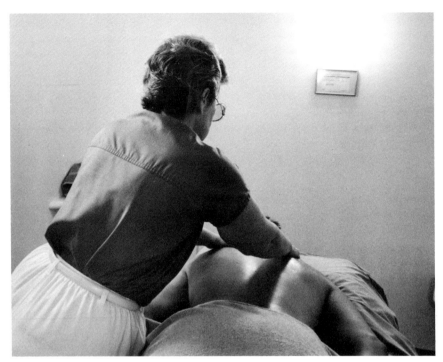
Kathy sometimes uses oils when giving a massage.

we use the serenity oils. If a guest is coming down with the flu, we use therapy oils. And when someone is feeling weak, we use vitality oils.

Fango is an Italian word meaning *mud*. Mud treatments are very popular in Europe. Here we use mud imported from Italy that has volcanic ash in it, which is rich in minerals and very therapeutic. I once worked on a lady who had suffered frostbite long ago. The only thing that ever gave her relief was the mud treatment.

HOW I GOT STARTED:
When I was a kid, my step-mother had a skin condition on her scalp and asked me to massage it. I enjoyed massaging her tremendously but never thought about pursuing massage as a career. Years later, a cousin of mine saw an ad for a massage school and suggested that I go. I knew right away that this was something that really interested me.

HOW I FEEL ABOUT IT:
I love my work. It's second nature to me now. Massage is one of the few jobs for which you get an instant response of appreciation and gratitude. And even when the guest doesn't say anything, I know I've made him or her

feel better. It may not be that instant, but because massage is therapeutic, I know it will make the person healthier in the long term. I really like the idea that I'm improving the health of our guests.

The one negative in this work is that massage professionals tend to get tendinitis as well as carpal tunnel syndrome, which affects the wrist. Any work that involves repetitive hand motions will do that to you. To protect yourself, you should do stretching exercises and get massages yourself. We give each other massages here at the spa.

WHAT YOU SHOULD KNOW:
If you're interested in this kind of work, find an accredited massage school in the state where you want to work. Each state has its own licensing system, and most states require a license for you to practice there legally. In school, you learn the history and techniques of massage, and you learn about anatomy and physiology.

The money varies from state to state. In Florida, working independently, you might earn an average of $50 an hour. Working as an employee at a health club, you might earn $20 per hour.

Kathy works to relieve the stress of the guests.

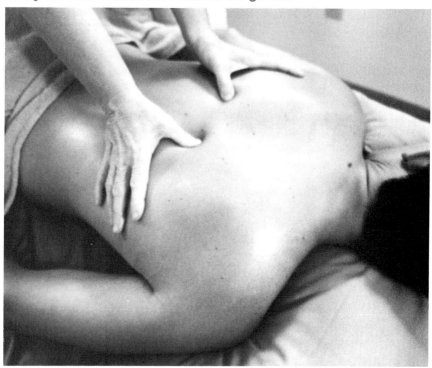

"Technology has changed
this business a lot, and we've
had to change with it."

JOHN LINDEMANN

LOCKSMITH

New York, New York

WHAT I DO:

I'm the manager of a locksmith company that installs and services locks. I used to go out into the field myself, but now I work in the shop taking calls from customers, many of whom are celebrities. I listen to their problems and send out servicemen to make the repairs. There are fifteen servicemen working here, and we cover all of Manhattan.

During a typical day, I'll answer calls from people who have all sorts of problems. Someone's locked his keys in his car. Someone's just moved to a new apartment and wants the locks changed. Or someone needs a broken lock repaired.

Servicing locks is a big part of this job. Sometimes we take the lock apart and replace worn-out springs.

John searches among his stock for the right key blank.

Old and worn-out parts are the most common problems we find, and they're usually with the lock, not the cylinder. People often confuse locks with cylinders. The lock is the part inside the door itself. The cylinder is the part that takes the key.

Technology has changed this business a lot, and we've had to change with it. Locks used to be made with pins inside the cylinders, but now they're being made with magnets instead. It's an entirely different kind of lock, and servicing it requires a different kind of education.

HOW I GOT STARTED:

I was working at a pharmacy next door to a locksmith's shop when I became friendly with the owner there. He asked me whether I'd be interested in learning the trade. I said yes, and he hired me. I worked for him for several years as an apprentice

59

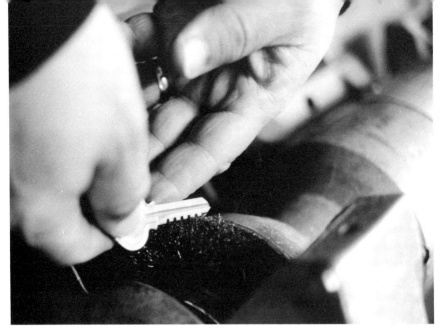

After the key is cut, John sands the rough edges.

before I moved to this shop, where I've been for twenty-five years.

HOW I FEEL ABOUT IT:

I really enjoy the challenge of coming across different types of locks that I haven't seen before. We deal with a lot of antique locks for which the keys have been lost. Trying to replace these old-fashioned keys is painstaking work, but it's also really interesting.

WHAT YOU SHOULD KNOW:

If you want to get into this business, work as an apprentice. Call locksmiths in your area and try to find someone who needs a hand. There are also correspondence locksmith courses, but I think they're a waste of time.

To do this work, you should be mechanically inclined and like to handle tools. But don't think that this is just manual work. Locksmiths also do a lot of work on computers. Let's say you need a key for a lock on a filing cabinet. First you find that lock's code number. Then you punch the code number into a computer. A program tells you the type of key blank that will fit the lock and tells the key machine how to cut that particular key. We do a lot of this type of work, especially with automobile locks.

The money can be quite good. As an apprentice, you might make around $250 a week. But once you're a full locksmith, you could earn up to $700 a week.

Related Careers

Here are more hands-on careers
you may want to explore:

ANTIQUES RESTORER
Antiques restorers return old pieces
of furniture, artwork, and jewelry to
their original state.

AUTOMOBILE MECHANIC
Automobile mechanics repair and
maintain cars.

ELECTRICIAN
Electricians install and repair
electrical equipment in office
buildings and homes.

ENGRAVER
Engravers etch metal plates that
are used in printing, including the
printing of postage stamps and
money.

ILLUSTRATOR
Illustrators draw art for
publications such as books and
magazines.

MAKE-UP ARTIST
Make-up artists create the make-up
for models, actors, and actresses
when they pose for photographs or
make film and stage appearances.

MUSICIAN
Musicians play instruments both
as soloists and in bands or
symphonies.

PET GROOMER
Pet groomers wash, brush, and clip
dogs, cats, and other domesticated
animals.

SCULPTOR
Sculptors are artists who create
three-dimensional works, such as
statues, from materials including
clay, metal, and wood.

UPHOLSTERER
Upholsterers cover chairs and sofas
with springs, padding, and fabric.

WATCHMAKER
Watchmakers make and repair the
clock mechanisms that allow
watches to keep time.

WELDER
Welders join pieces of metal, such as
pipes and machine parts, by heating
them and allowing the metal to
flow together.

Organizations

Contact these organizations for information
about the following careers:

VIDEOTAPE EDITOR
American Cinema Editors
1041 Formosa Avenue, West Hollywood, CA 90046

CHEF
American Culinary Federation
Box 3466, 10 San Bartola Avenue, St. Augustine, FL 32085

GRAPHIC ARTIST
American Institute of Graphic Arts
1059 Third Avenue, New York, NY 10021

CABINETMAKER
American Society of Furniture Designers
P.O. Box 2688, High Point, NC 27261

LOCKSMITH
Associated Locksmiths of America
3003 Live Oak Street, Dallas, TX 75204

GLASS ARTIST
Glass Art Society
Box 1364, Corning, NY 14830

GRAPHIC ARTIST
Graphic Arts Guild National
11 West 20th Street, New York, NY 10011

JEWELRY DESIGNER
Jewelers of America
1271 Avenue of the Americas, New York, NY 10020

HAT DESIGNER, TAILOR
National Association of Milliners, Dressmakers, and Tailors
157 West 126th Street, New York, NY 10027

BOOKBINDER
National Preservation Program
Library of Congress, Washington, DC 20540

MASONRY RESTORER
National Trust for Historic Preservation
614 H Street, N.W., Suite 305, Washington, DC 20001

GLASS ARTIST
Society of Glass and Ceramics Decorators
888 17th Street, N.W., Suite 600, Washington, DC 20006

Books

ART CAREER GUIDE
By Donald Holden. New York: Watson-Guptile Publications, 1983.

CAREERS ENCYCLOPEDIA
Homewood, Ill.: Dow-Jones Irwin, 1980.

CAREERS IN FILM AND VIDEO PRODUCTION
By Michael Honwin. Boston: Focal Press, 1990.

CAREERS IN TELEVISION
By Howard J. Blumenthal. New York: Little, Brown, 1992.

CREATIVE CAREERS
By Gary Blake and Robert W. Bly. New York: John Wiley, 1985.

DESIGN CAREERS
By Steven Heller and Lita Tolarico. New York: Van Nostrand
Reinhold, 1987.

THE ENCYCLOPEDIA OF CAREER CHOICES FOR THE 1990S
By Career Associates. New York: Walker, 1991.

GETTING INTO FASHION
By Melissa Jones. New York: Ballantine, 1984.

MAKING IT IN THE MEDIA PROFESSIONS
By Leonard Mogul. Chester, Ct.: Globe Pequot Press, 1987.

THE NEW YORK FINE ARTIST'S SOURCE BOOK
Division of Cultural Affairs of the City of New York. New York:
Addison-Wesley, 1983.

OCCUPATIONAL OUTLOOK HANDBOOK
Washington, D.C.: U.S. Department of Labor, 1990.

OFF BEAT CAREERS
By Al Sacharov. Berkeley, Ca.: Ten Speed Press, 1988.

THE SCHOOL OF VISUAL ARTS GUIDE TO CAREERS
By Dee Ito. New York: McGraw-Hill, 1987.

VGM'S CAREERS ENCYCLOPEDIA
Lincolnwood, Ill.: VGM Career Horizons, 1988.

Glossary Index